BUILDING BLOCKS OF MATH

OPERATIONS WITH WHOLE NUMBERS

Written by Regina Osweiller

Illustrated by Daniel Hawkins

WORLD BOOK

a Scott Fetzer company
Chicago

World Book, Inc.
180 North LaSalle Street
Suite 900
Chicago, Illinois 60601
USA

For information about other World Book publications,
visit our website at **www.worldbook.com**
or call **1-800-WORLDBK (967-5325)**.
For information about sales to schools and libraries,
call 1-800-975-3250 (United States),
or 1-800-837-5365 (Canada).

Library of Congress Cataloging-in-Publication Data
for this volume has been applied for.

Building Blocks of Math
ISBN: 978-0-7166-4253-4 (set, hc.)

Operations with Whole Numbers
ISBN: 978-0-7166-4260-2 (hc.)

Also available as:
ISBN: 978-0-7166-4270-1 (e-book)

1st printing June 2022

Acknowledgments:
Writer: Regina Osweiller
Illustrator: Daniel Hawkins/The Bright Agency
Colorist: Leo Trinidad/The Bright Agency
Series Advisor: Marjorie Frank
Special thanks to KnowledgeWorks Global Ltd.

TABLE OF CONTENTS

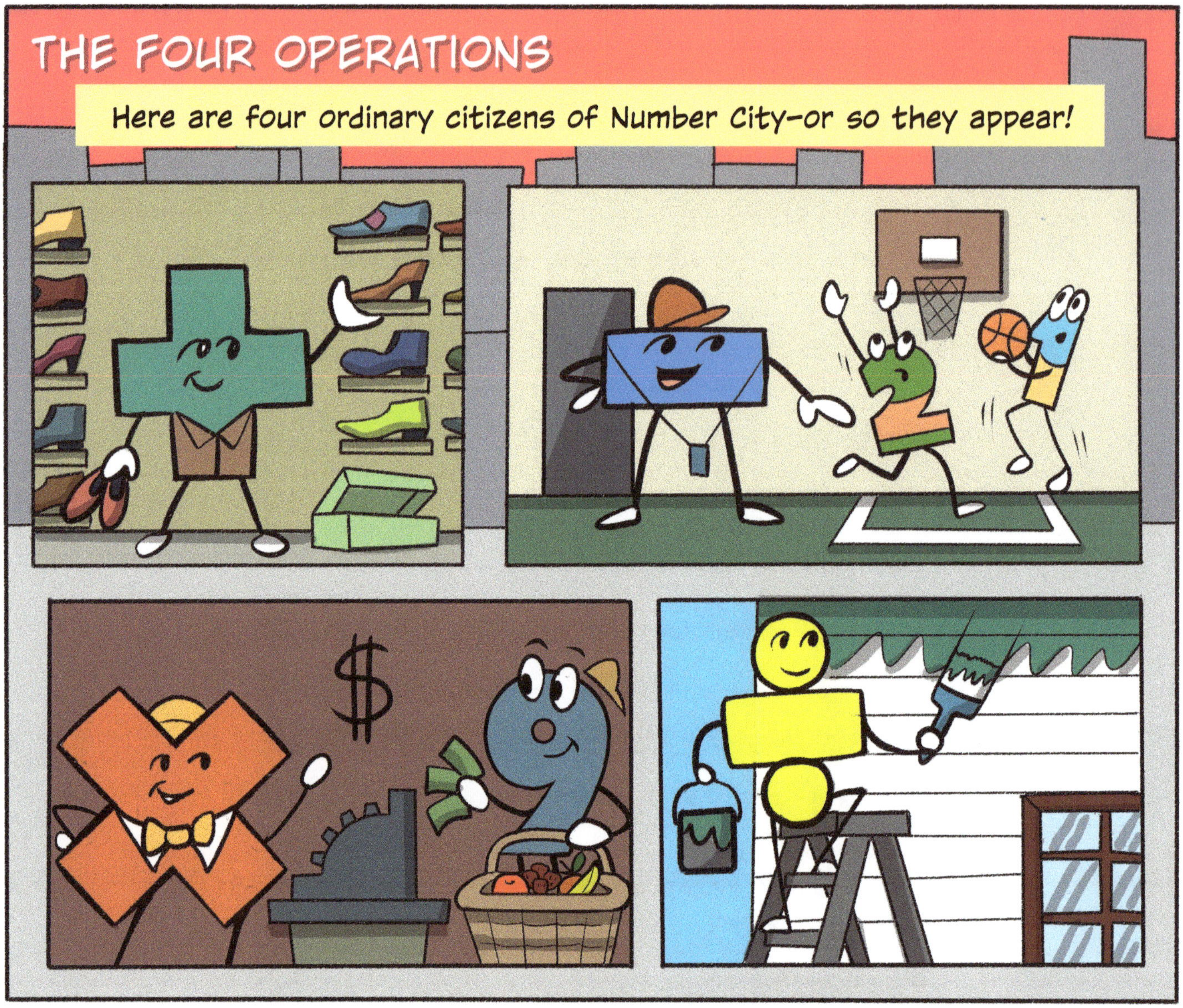

THE FOUR OPERATIONS

Here are four ordinary citizens of Number City—or so they appear!

THE OPERATIONS TEAM
I add numbers together!
BANK
$10
$1 $1 = $8
And I subtract numbers from one another!
I can multiply numbers with a cross, a dot, or parentheses! "6 x 5" is the same as 6 • 5, or 6(5).
I show one number divided by another. Sometimes I am a house!
POOF
Not that kind of house! A division house!
You can also be a fraction.
$30 \div 6 = 6\overline{)30} = \frac{30}{6}$
5

WORD CLUES ABOUT OPERATIONS

These words are clues that show which operation to use.
ALL TOGETHER, AND, IN ALL, SUM, TOTAL, INCREASE, BOTH
LESS, FEWER, HOW MANY MORE, DIFFERENCE, HOW MANY LEFT, DECREASE
TWICE, THREE TIMES, PRODUCT, DOUBLE, TIMES
DIVIDED BY, EQUAL SHARES, GIVE TO EACH, EQUAL PARTS, QUOTIENT

The difference between 24 and 17 is 7. Thank you, Minus Sign.
You're welcome! Can I get a free ticket to the game?
SCORE BOARD
EVENS
ODDS
24
17
7
AQUARIUM 
The tank now holds 15 fish. I just bought 8 more fish. How many fish in all?
"In all" you say? That's a clue to use addition!
15 + 8 = 23

What is the product of 8 and 11?

8 ☐ 11 = _____

What number is 12 less than 31?

31 ☐ 12 = _____

When 9 frogs join 28 frogs in a pond, how many frogs are in the pond all together?

9 ☐ 28 = _____

How can 91 centimeters of ribbon be shared evenly among 7 art projects?

91 ☐ 7 = _____

See page 40 for answers.

81
JUDGES
1ST ROUND SCORES
SKATER # (INPUT) | SCORE (OUTPUT)
3 | 27
5 | 45
8 | 72
9 | 81
Hmmm... Each score is related to the skater's number.
That's right! A function is a relationship between two groups of numbers, called an input and an output.
Each input has only one output. Functions can be shown on a function table. Here, the function rule involves an operation and a second number.
Can you find a rule for this function?
I see it! The final score for each of us is our skater number multiplied by 9! The rule is multiply by 9. What a coincidence!

SKATER # (INPUT)	SCORE (OUTPUT)
5	17
12	24
17	29
9	
18	
	32
	15

DANCER # (INPUT)	SCORE (OUTPUT)
72	57
45	30
50	35
31	
68	
	8
	41

INPUT	OUTPUT
46	23
50	25
8	4
12	6

RULE: MULTIPLY BY 3, AND ADD 1.

INPUT	OUTPUT
4	13
7	22
8	
11	

See page 40 for answers.

If I decrease by 8, and you are divided by 3, then I will be the greater number!
No, I will be greater!

This looks like a job for Minus Sign.
No, it's a job for Divided By!
Actually, we need both of you to solve this problem.
GRRR!

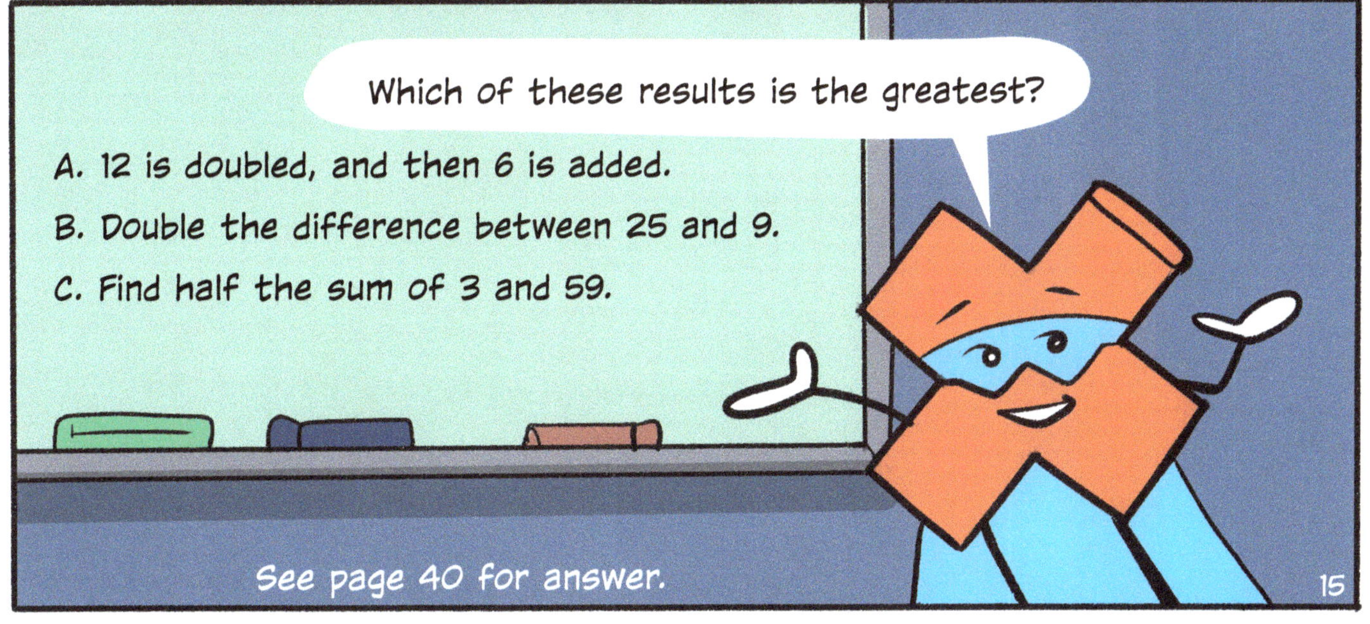

Use the clue words you learned on page 7 to use operations correctly.
33 DECREASED BY 8
↓
33 − 8
↓
25
72 DIVIDED BY 3
↓
72 ÷ 3
↓
24
25 is greater than 24, so I was right!
Which of these results is the greatest?
A. 12 is doubled, and then 6 is added.
B. Double the difference between 25 and 9.
C. Find half the sum of 3 and 59.
See page 40 for answer.

Plus Sign! Thank goodness you're here.
We want to know the total population of our two towns.
I can find the sum!
NUMBER CITY POP. 3,958
DIGIT TOWN POP. 2,013

Wait! A woman on Decimal Street just had twins, so our population has just gone up.
What's that? A family of four has left Digit Town for Rootville? That means our population has just gone down.

Um, can you guys settle on the numbers I'm supposed to add?

Hey, Plus Sign, don't sweat the fuzzy math. Check it out.
VROOOM!
To estimate is to choose a number that's close to the real answer. Choose numbers that are easy to use. You can use your rounding skills!
So, I will estimate the populations to the closest hundred.
POPULATION   ESTIMATE
3,958 → 4,000
2,013 → 2,000
TOTAL = 6,000
The sum of 6,000 is a good estimate of the combined population of both towns.
Estimation is especially helpful, since we aren't completely sure about the numbers we're adding.

I'd say there are 55 to 75 apples on each tree.

So how many apples does Farmer 11 have this year?

I count 11 trees. So I'll estimate 65 apples per tree, and round 11 down to 10.

65 x 10 equals 650. My estimate is 650 apples.

What will the new score be?

I'll round to the thousands place to estimate a score of 46,000 points and a penalty of 3,000 points.

FiSH QUEST

SCORE
45,887
PENALTY
2,915

So the estimate is 46,000 minus 3,000, or 43,000 points.

The fans are spread evenly among the 5 sections of the grandstands. How many fans are in each section?

ATTENDANCE
19,865

Round up the attendance to 20,000, and then divide by 5.

The estimate is 4,000 fans in each section.

EXPONENTS
Meanwhile, something unusual is happening at the Trampoline Park.
Three! What's happening to you?
SNACKS
PARK
ZAP!
I ... I don't know! I seem to be stuck in the air, and a little smaller. What could that mean?

It means you're now an exponent!
BWA-HAH HAH-HAH!
And you, Ms. Two, I changed you into a base!
What are bases and exponents?

See page 40 for answers.

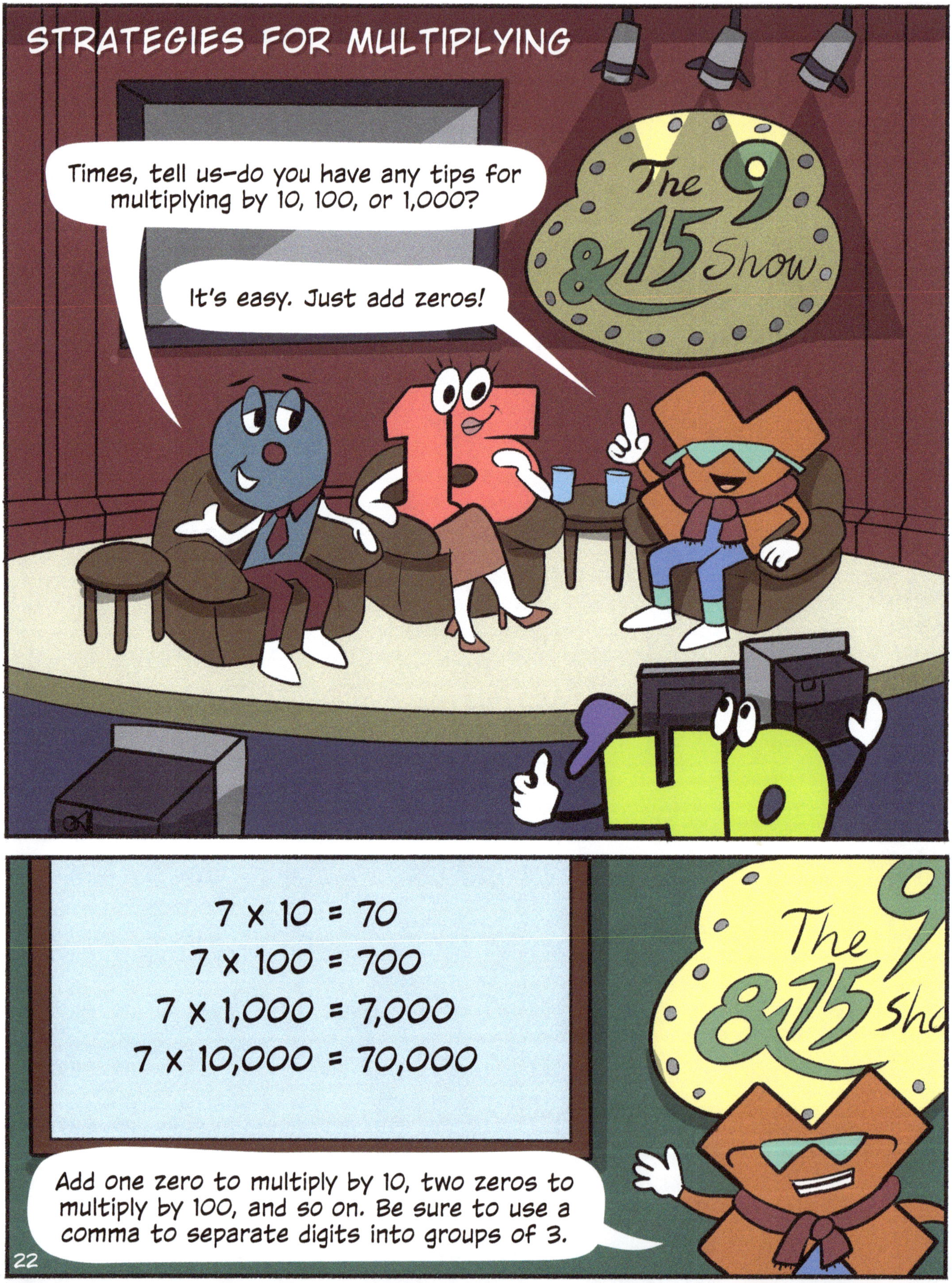

STRATEGIES FOR MULTIPLYING

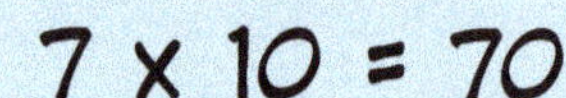

But how can you multiply by 40, which is a multiple of 10? A **multiple** is a whole number product of another number.

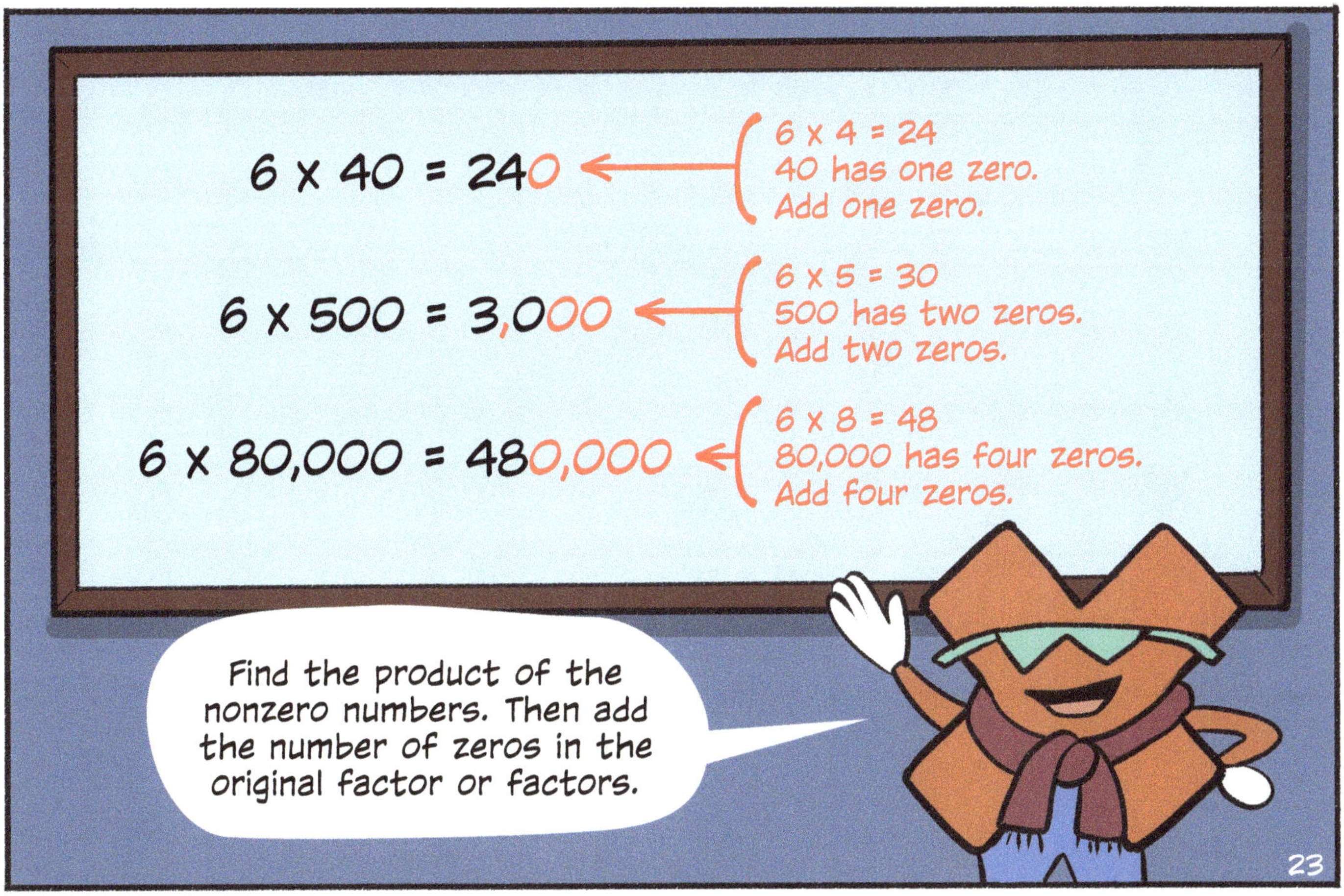

6 × 40 = 24**0**

6 × 4 = 24
40 has one zero.
Add one zero.

6 × 500 = 3,0**00**

6 × 5 = 30
500 has two zeros.
Add two zeros.

6 × 80,000 = 48**0,000**

6 × 8 = 48
80,000 has four zeros.
Add four zeros.

Find the product of the nonzero numbers. Then add the number of zeros in the original factor or factors.

STRATEGIES FOR DIVIDING

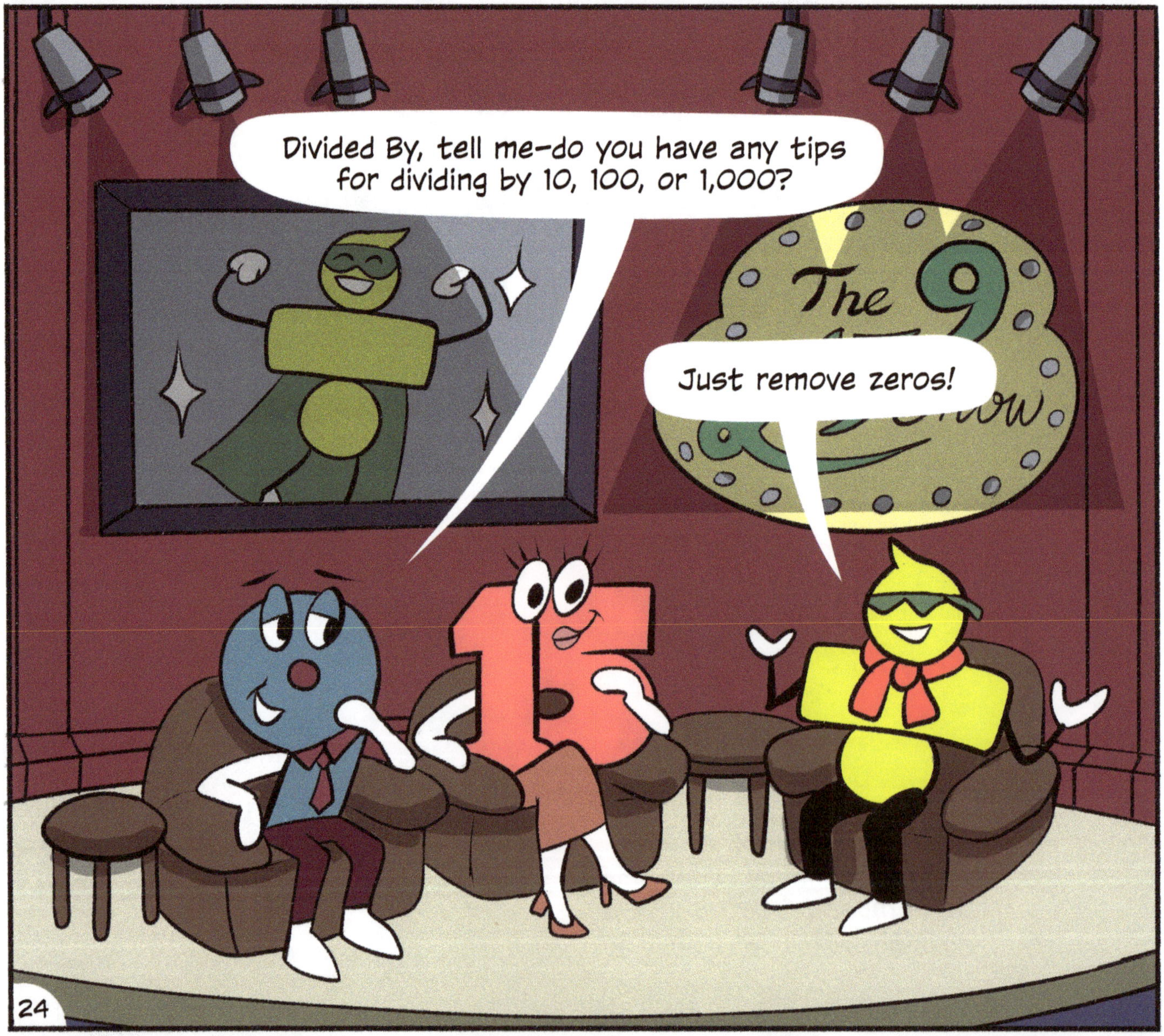

Remove one zero to divide by 10, two zeros to divide by 100, and so on. Be sure to use a comma to separate the digits into groups of 3.

You stole the second part of that from me!

8,400 ÷ 10 = 840

9,500 ÷ 100 = 95

318,000 ÷ 1,000 = 318

TELEPROMPTER

EXIT

Remove the same number of zeros from the larger number (the dividend). Then solve the problem.

8,400 ÷ 20 = 840 ÷ 2 = 420
(one zero removed from divisor and dividend)

9,500 ÷ 500 = 95 ÷ 5 = 19
(two zeros removed)

318,000 ÷ 3,000 = 318 ÷ 3 = 106
(three zeros removed)

LIVE AUDI

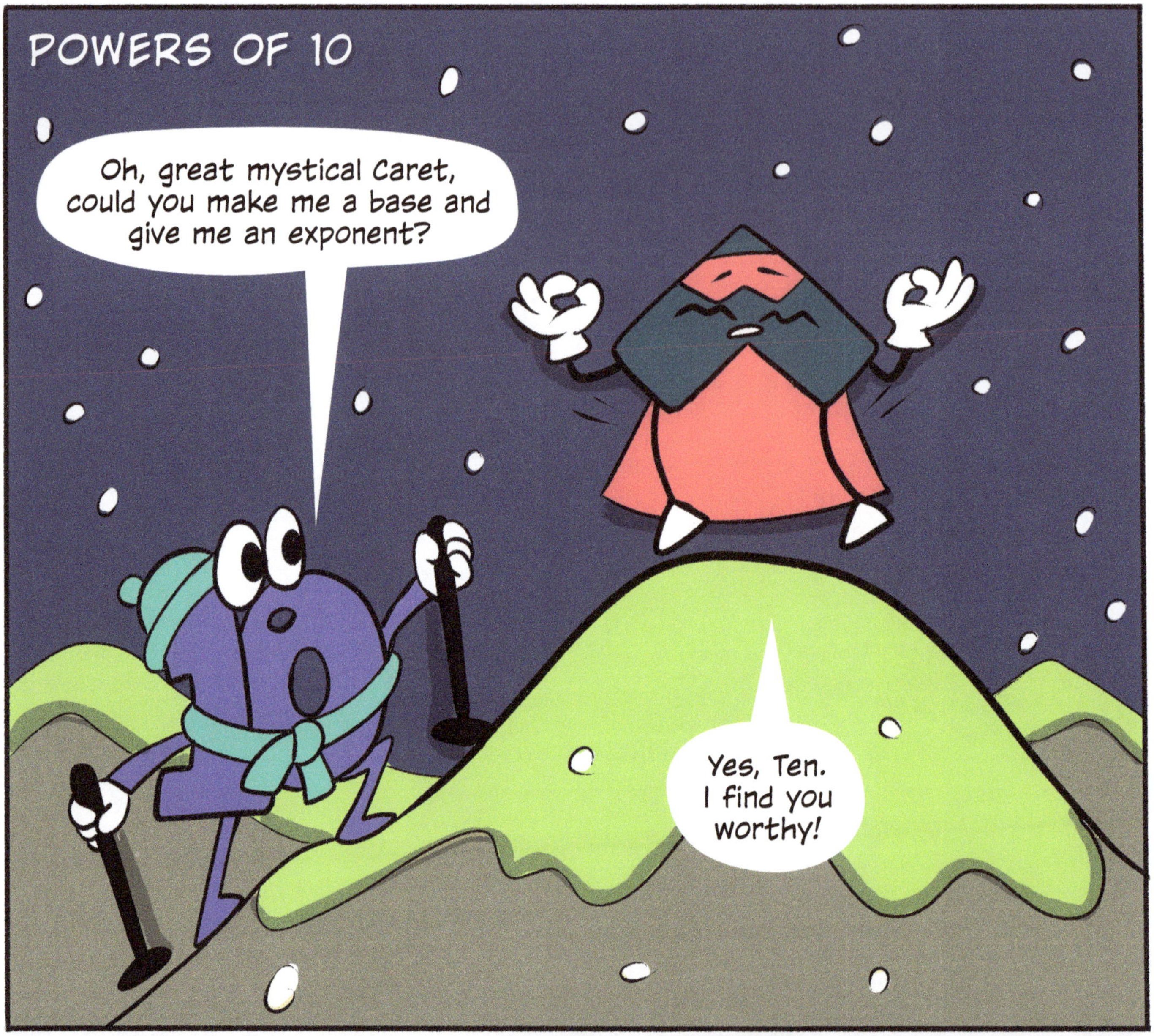

Oh, great mystical Caret, could you make me a base and give me an exponent?
Yes, Ten. I find you worthy!
Remember, my presence means that a base is raised to the power shown by an exponent.

Distance of a round trip to the International Space Station: 10^3 kilometers
Mass of the moon: 10^{24} kilograms
Shortest round trip, Earth to Mars: 10^8 kilometers
$10^4 = 10 \times 10 \times 10 \times 10 = 10{,}000$
$10^3 = 10 \times 10 \times 10 = 1{,}000$
$10^2 = 10 \times 10 = 100$
$10^1 = 10$
Behold, these numbers are **powers** of 10!
This means that 10 is the base and whole number next to it is the exponent.
The exponent tells the number of zeros in the standard number. For example, 10^3 means 10 to the third power, shown with 3 zeros.

MENTAL MATH

Welcome to my lair. I'm here to teach you about **mental math**, which is math you can do all in your head. You don't need paper, pencil, or a calculator.
Of course, sometimes it's okay to jot things down when you're doing mental math.

To find the sum of two-digit numbers, add the place values. The two cans have a total of 141 Calories.
45 + 96
40 + 90 = 130
5 + 6 = 11
SUM: 141
45 CALORIES
96 CALORIES
MILK

I'm ahead 115 to 95. How many points do you need to catch up?
I can subtract by adding. I ask, how many more points does it take to make 115? The answer is 20 more points.
115 - 95
115 = 95 + ?
? = 20

I already have 387 cat toys, and now I have 9 more.
Use the 9 trick, which is to add 10 and then subtract 1.
Adding 10 gives me 397. Subtract 1, and now I have 396 cat toys.
387 + 9
387 + 10 − 1 = 397 − 1 = 396
9 CAT TOYS

How many dots in all?
397 Dots
36 Dots
Break apart the smaller number to form compatible numbers, which are numbers that are easy to add. It's easy to add 3 to 397. So I'll break 36 into 33 + 3. There are 433 dots in all.
397 + 36
397 + 3 + 33 = 400 + 33 = 433

We have already driven 68 kilometers. How far will we travel today?
Make a ten by adding a small number. Then subtract that small number from the other addend.
COOLVILLE 17 km

68 + 17
(68 + 2) + (17 - 2)
= 70 + 15
= 85
We'll travel 85 kilometers.

REASONABLENESS

I have 358 strawberries and the space creature is staying for 12 days.
So, can I eat 20 strawberries a day?
Hmmm. We can round 358 up to 360, then find 360 divided by 12 is equal to 30. So, the space creature can eat almost 30 strawberries a day if it wants to.
Yeah!

The length of the Great Wall is more than 20,000 kilometers.
We can walk 20 kilometers in a day. So we can walk the whole wall in 100 days, or about 3 months, right?
GUIDE BOOK
Sorry, no, that's not a reasonable answer. 20 x 100 is equal to 2,000, not 20,000. To walk the Great Wall you'll need 1,000 days, which is about 3 years.

TALENT SHOW

We have 17 acts, and the show can't last longer than 120 minutes. How much time can I give to each act?

6 × 17 = 102
7 × 17 = 119

Look at the multiples of 17. If each act takes 7 minutes, then the show will be 119 minutes long.

Maybe, but that leaves only 1 minute to spare. You'll need time to introduce the acts and get them on stage.

I think 6 minutes for each act is more reasonable.

CONCLUSION

I'm proud of all of you! You really showed your knowledge of operations, and you helped the good people of Number City.

Calling the Operations Team. Are you there? We have a problem and need your help.

We're all here, Mayor—and we're ready for anything!

2x-y
x^2-2x+4
$x^2(3x+y)$
+5y
3x+2y-8
7x
10(xy)
$a^2+2ab+b^2$
3z-w
x+y
$(a^2+a) \div a$
4a(3b)
Good. Take a look at this.

Tune in for the next exciting adventure of ... the Operations Team!

SHOW WHAT YOU KNOW

1. What number is 4 less than 24? _______   A. 24 ÷ 4 = 6

2. What is the product of 24 and 4? _______   B. 24 + 4 = 28

3. What number is the quotient of 24 and 4? _______   C. 24 − 4 = 20

4. What is the sum of 24 and 4? _______   D. 24 x 4 = 96

Input	Output
13	45
21	53
5	37
26	
38	
	56
	85

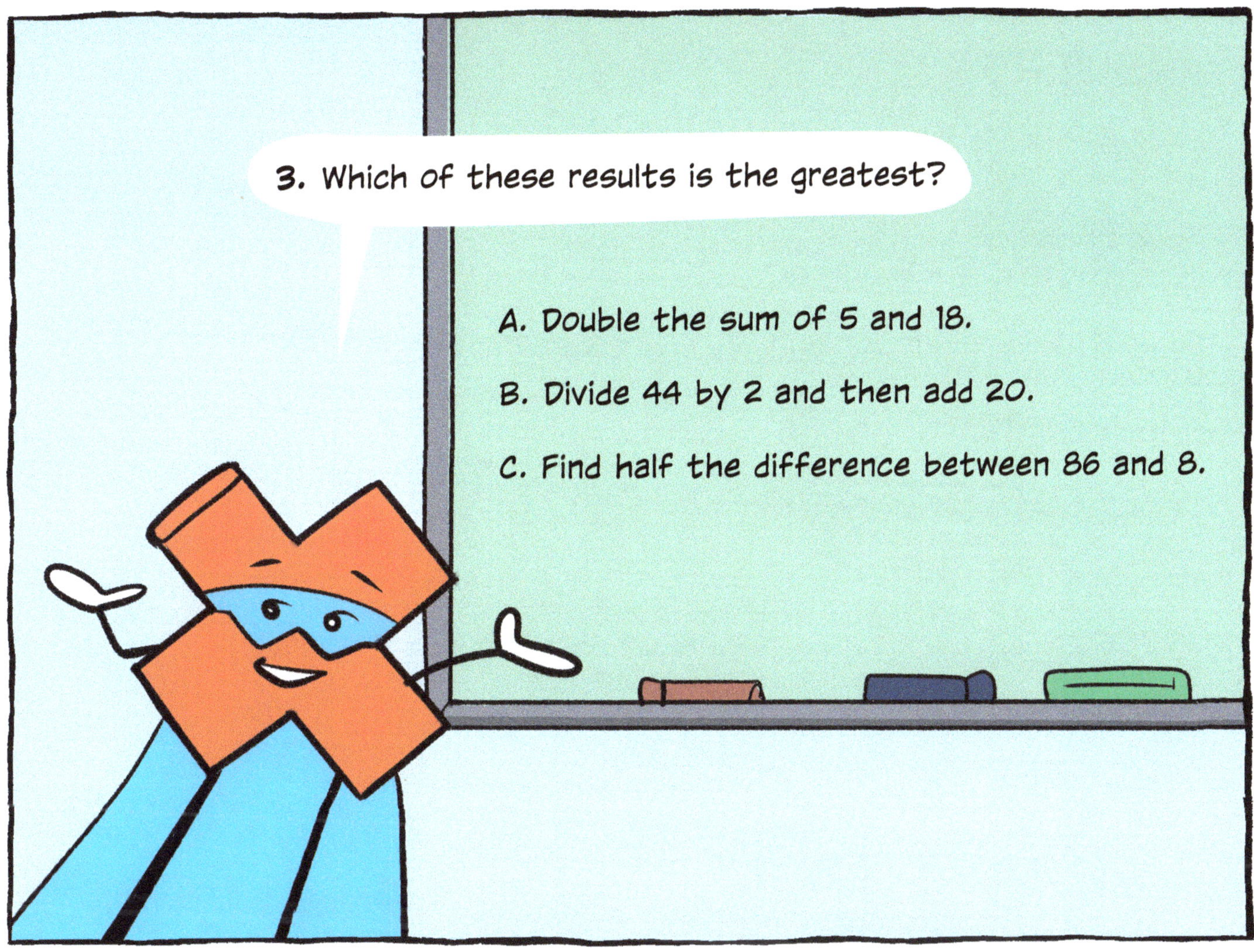

4. **Multiple choice.** Let's see how well you can answer these questions involving exponents.

1. Which of these numbers equals 10^4?
   A. 1,000
   B. 10,000
   C. 100,000

2. Which of these numbers equals 3^3?
   A. 3
   B. 9
   C. 27

3. What number does x represent in this problem: $81 = 3^x$?
   A. 3
   B. 4
   C. 9

4. What number does x represent in this problem: $32 = 2^x$?
   A. 5
   B. 7
   C. 16

See page 40 for answers.

ANSWERS

Page 9: 8 x 11 = 88; 31 - 12 = 19; 9 + 28 = 37; 91 ÷ 7 = 13

Page 11: Missing skater numbers: 20, 3; Missing scores: 21, 30

Page 12: Rule: Subtract 15 Missing dancer numbers: 23, 56; Missing scores 16, 53

Page 13: First table: Divide by 2; Second table: Missing: 25, 34

Page 15: A. 30, B. 32, C. 31, so B. is greatest.

Page 21: $n = 5$; $x = 6$

SHOW WHAT YOU KNOW ANSWERS pages 38-39:

1.
1. C. 24 - 4 = 20. The word "less" is a clue for subtraction.
2. D. 24 x 4 = 96. The word "product" is a clue for multiplication.
3. A. 24 ÷ 4 = 6. The word "quotient" is a clue for division.
4. B. 24 + 4 = 28. The word "sum" is a clue for addition.

2.

Input	Output
13	45
21	53
5	37
26	**58**
38	**70**
24	56
53	85

Add 32 to each number in the input column to get the number in the output column.

3.
A. First, add 5 + 18 = 23. Next, multiply 23 x 2 = 46.
B. First divide 44 ÷ 2 = 22. Next, add 22 + 20 = 42.
C. First subtract 86 - 8 = 78. Next divide 78 ÷ 2 = 39.
Result A is the greatest.

4.
1. The number 10,000 (B) equals 10^4 (10 x 10 x 10 x 10 = 10,000).
2. The number 27 (C) equals 3^3 (3 x 3 x 3 = 27).
3. The x represents the number 4 (B) because $3^4 = 81$ (3 x 3 x 3 x 3 = 81).
4. The x represents the number 5 (A) because $2^5 = 32$ (2 x 2 x 2 x 2 x 2 = 32).